T0082772

Raw, Real, Recovering

Exploring Healing through Others' Life Lessons

LYNETTE SINGLETON

RAW, REAL, RECOVERING
EXPLORING HEALING THROUGH OTHERS' LIFE LESSONS

iUniverse books may be ordered through booksellers or by contacting:

iUniverse
1663 Liberty Drive
Bloomington, IN 47403
www.iuniverse.com
844-349-9409

ISBN: 978-1-6632-1212-2 (sc)
ISBN: 978-1-6632-1213-9 (e)

Library of Congress Control Number: 2020921109

Print information available on the last page.

iUniverse rev. date: 10/30/2020

Contents

Introduction

I'm a healed soul. Through my healing began my love of writing poetry simply to share my truth about my own healing. Out of therapy, prayer, and leaning on close friends, a small collection of poems was birthed. Had no intentions of publishing, but guided by God, I decided to follow what was inspired with others' gentle encouragement. I truly pray these poems touch someone and journey has inspired someone, anyone, even if only one. Thank you to my family (all of you) and my friends (you know who you are).

God willing and God bless.

Me

Born July 21, 1968,
to her parents; what an exciting day.
Their first child, two young parents so much promise to come,
wait three years later, now they're having a son.
Some would say they're living the dream—
got the family, the house.
Two years later, divorce and no spouse.
Family is broken; drag the children to a home they don't know.
New man in the picture says the kids got to go.
So much anger; Mom, can't you say a word?
Not really sure why, maybe her own childhood.
Through the years, three states we moved, spent only summers with Dad.
Each time I left him broke my heart to see him so sad.
Fast-forward, first boyfriend, now pregnant as a teen.
Had abortion killed my self-esteem.
Speed ahead, now I'm twenty in Atlanta, new life.
Had another baby before I'm a wife.
Best moment in my life—giving birth to my son.
Now his father and I perhaps life's now begun.
No, a series of breakups; two years later, we're married.
Second child on the way; will this baby be carried
successfully with a mom and a dad?
No, broke up again. This time I'm truly sad.
Determined, on my own with two small kids to raise.
Late nights need relief from the struggle most days.
Caught up with new friends; drugs, all-night parties begin.
Now begins many of my new sins.
My life begins a downward spiral.
Confiding in my husband, he was not in denial.
Just gave his life to the Lord.

God saved him to save me just in time.
My life now became an uphill climb.
Took some time … now
baby number 3.
So glad that God showed me how happy I could be
to share my pregnancy with my husband at last.
Now a family in California; can we stay on task?
With God's help and His blessings and grace,
our kids are now grown; thank God that's the case.
Twenty-nine years of marriage with pain, tears, and joy
could have been a different story with a life destroyed.
Instead, I'm still writing; my story's not over.
Still living my dash, wearing my glorified, God-given sash.
It's just me living my life the best I can be … Just me!

Chapter 1

Raw

1. World Unspoken

The love that I have received, it's so young,
before I even knew what love really was.
We grew up together, brokenness feeding broken.
We learned to navigate through this world unspoken.
Couldn't ever imagine you gone from my life;
imagined the day you would make me your wife.
Then challenges came, and I wanted out
before I even knew what life was about.
Did you know me, feel me, even understand?
I was a child, and I made you my man.
Pieces of a dad in my life I knew not,
not what it even meant to receive what I got.
Needed so much healing myself, and now we have kids.
What to do to navigate through a marriage too soon?
But you know my past, all I've been through.
All I wanted was you to make my dreams true.
I had to learn to let God heal my soul,
And accept His gift was my goal.
I still ride with you and you, me.
The scars in our past still show up; let them be.
Understanding the scars makes us stronger.
Can we go the distance just a little way longer.
We won't stop till our last breath, baby; we've come this far,
let me be the healing to your scar.
Let's comfort each other till death do us part,
get all God's promises; let's not miss the mark.
We grew up together—broken feeding broken—
and navigated through this world unspoken.

2. Picked by Design

I may not have picked you to be the one for me,
but God designed this, you see.
We were picked by design,
paired with love in His eyes,
set out to win that famous prize—
to be together at last
despite what's been done in our past.
He knew it, we didn't; the plan was laid out,
even thought we had no idea what it was about.
You wouldn't have chosen this path you are on
or the journey, my love.
Thought you'd be gone.
You saw long before me the plan God laid out.
You were obedient and stayed faithful, even though you had doubts.
God saved you in time to save me.
Forever grateful to you I'll be.
We were picked by design, neither one of our plans.
I'm proud to call you my man.

3. Awkward Silence

Awkward silence most of the time
Due to unresolved issues we've had over time.
Living together, trying to exist,
Day after day, awkwardness persists.
Trust seemed dissolved,
Little resolved.
What's happened? Look what's evolved.
Around most people we seem okay.
Until they're all gone, and we go back the same way.
I try to hold on to memories we've made.
Seems more difficult to remember what we gave.
Me and you the energy to carry through,
Is it possible to make this love feel brand new?

4. The Life That Was Promised (Tribute to CA)

The life that was promised from the time I remembered
doesn't look like the life that resembled
that silver lining my grandma told me.
Instead, what showed up is the life that you see.
Four children, no husband, struggling to survive, and many of my church friends only criticize
my life as they see it; if only
they knew
this wasn't the life that I choose.
So many also say, "I see all good in you."
But the pain in my life, in my childhood, there was nothing they knew.
Trying to repair all the hurt and abuse
that was caused from a family member shattered my youth.
He broke the law,
but no charges were brought because I didn't confess
to a family I felt like couldn't care less.
So today, as a mother, I want more for my babies.
But it seems God is the only one with the keys
to reverse the past and set me free.
So I find myself constantly on my knees,
Praying, "Lord, deliver me from the past.
Change the course of my history at last.
Use my pain for good to change those you love.
I surrender my love to God above."

5. Page from Her Book (Tribute to J)

As my very last child, God gave me a daughter.
Best time in my life, just like life started over.
I like to think that she saved my life,
came out of addiction, and then was saved by Christ.
Put Grace in her name, at the stage I was in,
coming so deep, so deep out of sin.
I knew, I just knew His grace he gave to carry this child.
Longest labor yct, far, far from mild.
Over sixteen hours in order to give birth.
She came in the world, and I've seen all the worth
in her eyes, her face so soft to the touch.
Ms. Grace, I love you so much.
Through the years, as she grew into a young teen,
voices she heard and faces she saw.
Got help and therapy to discover the truth.
They prescribed meds to help with the root
cause of what was happening in her mind.
Said we'd have to wait and see, just give it time.
Graduation had a party, plans for college,
all of that changed given the knowledge.
We found her very distant, estranged, stayed in her room.
The challenge we had affected her mind.
Very tough months ahead of us now.
The scriptures I knew had to be read out loud, sometimes yelling and crying; so much time spent on my knees.
Lord, deliver my child; You can do it with ease.
Over time, God brought comfort, showed Himself as almighty.
Time after time, He's shown Himself brightly.
Diagnosis is real, but what God did show me
was this wouldn't keep her from being all she can be.

This child … God blessed me with the most incredible girl.
Can't tell you how much she cares for people in this world.
Most caring and giving and thoughtful bright light,
she gives so unselfishly to all in her sight.
Expresses through music, talented and gifted; when she sings, folks' spirts are lifted.
Yes, there are hard days, her battle sometimes daily.
But she doesn't give up.
Through her life I take a page from her book
to be strong, be faithful, and trust in the God above.
His plans are perfect, and it's you that He loves.
I end my words now, and I think this much you knew,
this mom, baby girl, is really proud of you.

6. Did You Know?

Did you know you weren't born in this world by yourself?
Self-righteous acts prove maybe you don't.
Did you know there's a Golden Rule we should live by?
Treat others more highly then self, and don't lie.
Did you know they're real lessons in life we should learn?
If not learned, it matters, and it's a concern.
See, your actions have real consequences that affect everyone,
over seven billion folks under the sun.
It's not just you in this life alone ; did you know? If so it should show?
Remember this, you will indeed reap what you sow.
Did you know your not in this life alone?

7. Beauty and Darkness

I see beauty all around me, and darkness and light.
I see love and hate all in my mind; that's the fight.
These opposites really exist;
contradictions in life, they really exist.
I choose right over wrong,
truth over lies.
Being tossed to and fro I really despise.
Our humanist and the struggle
between good and bad, this is the life that we have.
A choice God gave us, the chance to choose.
Oh, that we would honor Him and not abuse
these privileges that are given to us.
Come let us reason and discuss.
Bring these talks to the table; shed light on what's hard.
Calculate our errors and ways that we bombard.
And perhaps one day we'll get over these scars,
stains, and struggles that really exist,
and the sins in our lives that continue and persist.
Live each day with new mercies in what God says.
I see beauty all around me, and darkness in my head.

Chapter 2

Real

8. Truth You Tell Us

The lies we tell ourselves in our head
while lying at night alone in our bed.
I'm not good enough, strong enough; I've disappointed so many.
Should have done so much more with my life; I've had plenty,
plenty of time to get it right.
But mistakes I repeat over and over, day and night.
Feel as if I'm constantly asking God to forgive.
These sins, here you take them; make them not exist.
Find myself repeating the same prayer over and over:
"Lord Jesus, take the wheel. Come, please make me
into the person you created me to be.
I desperately want to see
what she looks like, acts like, walks like, talks like.
The lies we tell ourselves aren't real.
But your Word is the truth and will allow us to heal.
Thank you for the truth you tell us and for the Word that molds us."

9. I'll Remember
(Tribute for My Friend X)

You were taken too soon from the life we just started.
Now death separates us, once here now departed.
Find myself asking why since you were my love.
I singled you out cuz you fit like a glove
to my body, my soul, and especially my mind.
I prided myself you were one of a kind.
No one else got me, touched me so deeply.
The way you were taken robbed me so cheaply.
Had to figure out how to make it each day
and go without that touch you gave in such a special way.
No one can replace you and the friendship we had.
I'm teaching our child these memories of her dad.
Yet still my heart breaks about all that could be,
raising our family, and now it's just me.
It's been so many years now since you have passed,
but the memories of your touch will always last.
For eternity, my man, I'll always remember this life that I started
with you, still brokenhearted.
Every memory we held close to heart,
my beloved, my love won't depart. I'll remember.

10. Love so Rare

This love that we share, I'll just say it's so rare.
So unexpected till one day I knew.
Couldn't ignore it any longer; it had to be you.
When we first met, yeah you caught my eye.
But real talk, wasn't lookin' for a guy.
Been in relationships I could say were complicated.
Felt as though 'cause of that, okay, yeah I was jaded.
Only wanted a friendship, so we hung out as friends.
How in the world did this whirlwind begin?
Couldn't imagine the day that I'd be your wife.
The day you proposed was the shock of my life.
And there was no way I couldn't say yes.
It's with you I felt my best.
Thank you for loving me with all your heart.
What the Lord put together no one can depart.
From now until were old and gray,
I cherish this day and forever … so rare.

11. The Skin You're In

The skin that you're in is a gift, but we wise
some despise, so wear it with pride.
Hold your head up high.
God designed you uniquely with love in His eyes
and gave you a gift to use to bring Him glory.
Share your story!
Put trust in the One that created,
letting Him handle the hate and the hated.
Every hair on your head it was counted.
Your life was purposed and planned before you were conceived.
Do you believe?
You are incredibly loved.
Do you believe?
Christ died for you, shed His blood for you, rose, and intercedes for you.
He's forgiven you!
Do you believe?
Feel good in the skin that you're in!

11.a. The Skin You're In Part II

So, you say your confused bout 'the skin that you are in, why do you think that is?
Maybe you've lived life by someone's mindsets, well I tell you that's none of their biz, …
People pleasing all the time, its front and a falsehood, will the real please stand up right now,
While your unrecognizable to you on the outside, inside your screaming out loud,
Victorious in your own head but no one can hear you shout "I'm here can't you see me" I'm here!
Can anyone see my internal fear?
No instead what you see is only a shell…. cause I'm scared and afraid, so I show someone else
… on the outside it's not real what you see…
But I know comes a day when I'll truly be me
There's a pain that I feel speaking words that aren't mine, acting intelligent most of the time,
When I know I betray a portion of the real – from others life I do steal, a little of this and a little of that
Picking up phrases from many I've sat, at the feet listening wishing I could be someone other than me.
Why am I so uncomfortable in the skin that I'm in – wanting to be so much more …. maybe because I know the sin that's within– inside and I wanted to sore…. Above where I am it's others life's I adore.
Today In the mirror I look, smile at what I see, shake my head check again and now I believe – this is me in my skin – now others can see hold me accountable at being just me….
So, you say you were confused 'bout the skin that your in…. no more it's your time - now life truly begins!

If you want it don't try to be someone you're not, be authentically you its this life you got… got it show it – the true self if others don't like it …. Well, its ok ………….
You - feel good in the skin that you're in….

Chapter 3

Recovering

12. You Have Permission

You have permission
to love yourself,
forgive yourself, admire yourself,
be yourself, free yourself
from the hate you give yourself.
Rest in the knowledge of the Creator who made you.
Seek God's wisdom
He designed you
and loves you,
loves you unconditionally, and chose you.
Tomorrow is not promised; the past is the past.
Live in this moment; eternity is what lasts.
Our home is not here;
it's being designed in God's eyes.
While we're here on this earth, let us not compromise
the truth that He's given.
Let go of the sin that holds ourselves hostage.
Release, let life in.
You have permission.

13. The Peak

It's a long road up to climb in your mind to tell yourself, "Don't be weak."
But the mountain you're climbing does have a peak.
When you stand at the top, lift your hands to the sky.
Now look down, see the bottom, and know that you survived.
Every step that you took to get up to the top
was a lesson you learned; no, you never stopped.
Got bruises and scrapes, maybe even shed some blood.
Even fell down and got your face in the mud.
Picked yourself up, cleaned off, took one more step.
Then some sunlight halfway with bright days gave you pep,
and energy to keep climbing with the top in reach.
Add some prayer and God's Word, and Jesus to teach.
Here we go; got momentum, and my climb's almost done.
This weight that I'm carrying truly weighs a ton.
Shed some pounds, now I'm feeling quite lean.
Look out, world, I'm coming, sight unseen.
It's a long road to climb in mind not to be weak.
These are the words I speak.
That mountain ahead does have a peak.

14. Story to Tell

It's your story to tell.
Don't let anyone else write it.
The future is now; it's your fight, now fight it.
Set the example, pave the path for others to follow.
Have regrets?
Repent, there's always tomorrow.
God willing; it's His will to give life or take it.
He knows all, no need to half step and fake it.
He has a plan; be still, wait, and see.
Jesus told us in His Word, "Come follow me."
Share your story with pride; you don't know who it will bless.
Maybe someone who's out there, grief-stricken and stressed.
That very story may just save a life—perhaps someone abused, fed up, in strife.
You may be the tool God chooses to use.
Those battles you're in will show every bruise.
Don't be shy or ashamed of the life you've lived in the past.
Show the true you, and remove the mask.
The design God created, no one else's is the same.
He loves you so much; that's just why He came
and died and rose, interceding for you.
That story you're telling can make someone's life new.
It's a testimony blessed by the Creator,
and He is the one and only originator.
From sunset to sunrise each day brings new mercies to see.
Take a look in the mirror and say, "Thank God for me
and my story."
It's only yours to tell.
Now go out and tell it!

15. Standing Firm

My healings began; no stopping me now.
Your words don't bother; no way I'll allow
what you say to effect me in a negative way.
Won't ever happen, not where I stand today.
Now my path is victorious; no stopping me now.
Applause, applause, let me take a bow.
Defeat's not an option; I stand on God's book.
He truly loves me, gave all that it took.
I now know my worth, feeling quite fine
to know I'm uniquely designed.
Go on with those words brining up my past,
so far behind me at last.
I've learned from mistakes; no one holds me down.
I'm standing with both feet on the ground.
Solid foundation, no shakiness now,
accepting forgiveness, I vow.
Thankful for psalms and what David says too,
bearing with one another, and Christ forgives you.
Need approval of God and no one else, this I've learned.
I stand on my God's truth that is firm.

Printed in the United States
By Bookmasters